Contents

© 1997 Summy-Birchard Music, a division of Summy-Birchard Inc.
Exclusive print rights administered by Alfred Music. All rights reserved. Printed in USA.
ISBN 0-87487-762-8

A Note to Students

The pieces in this book have been specially designed to help you find certain important notes (I call them "targets") on the cello fingerboard. The notes that I think of as targets have the same names as the open strings. That way, I can always be sure I have hit the "bull's eye" by testing the fingered note with an open string. These pieces also help you to learn how certain other notes are easy to play once you have hit the target. For example, if you are very good at hitting G on the D-string with 2nd finger, then G-sharp (even though it sounds rather ominous) is very easy to play with third finger.

In order to get the most out of this book, there are a few things you should do:

• You should play the top line of all the duets.

• Listen carefully and play well in tune. Notice all of the times when a target note is played before or after an open string with the same name. Be sure they match!

• Know the names of all of the notes you are playing. It is important that you know the name of the target note. Then you must know the names of the notes which "live next door" under the other fingers on the same string. It is also important to know the names of the notes which "live across the street" on the other strings in the same position.

• In many of the pieces, you will play the target note before playing any of the "neighbors". In others, you will have to play a neighboring note before playing the target note. In still others, you will never actually play the target note (in these cases I think of the targets as being "invisible" -- that is, the target is still there but you don't hear it.) Please notice that in *all* of these circumstances you should think about the target note to find your place on the fingerboard whether you play it first, second, or never!

• You will notice that some of the fingerings are written in for you and some are not. However you should remember that I always put in a fingering if it is necessary for you to shift. So if you do *not* see a finger number, you should assume that you do *not* have to shift -- you must figure out how to play the notes without moving your hand.

• As you are practicing these pieces, pay close attention to how it feels to hit the targets. You have to able to hit them accurately and consistently (without looking at your hand, of course) -- and you must know if the notes are correct *before* you hear them played. If you learn the feeling of hitting the targets with different fingers, then you can play many other notes without difficulty.

Above all, have fun playing the pieces!

-- Rick Mooney

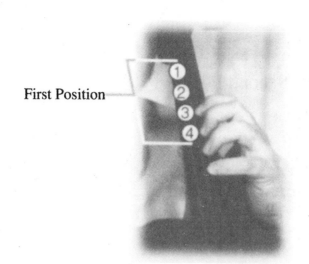

First Position

"Upper" Second Position

Target Practice

Geography Quiz

Your 2nd finger is on D on the A-string. Answer the following questions:

What note will be played by:

1 on the A-string? ____

3 on the A-string? ____

What is another
name for that note? ____

4 on the A-string? ____

2 on the D-string? ____

2 on the G-string? ____

2 on the C-string? ____

3 on the D-string? ____

What is another
name for that note? ____

What finger will you use to play:

E♭ on the A-string? ____

A on the D-string? ____

C on the G-string? ____

G on the C-string? ____

F♯ on the D-string? ____

F♯ on the C-string? ____

B on the G-string? ____

E on the C-string? ____

D♭ on the A-string? ____

4

Names and Numbers
"Upper" Second Position

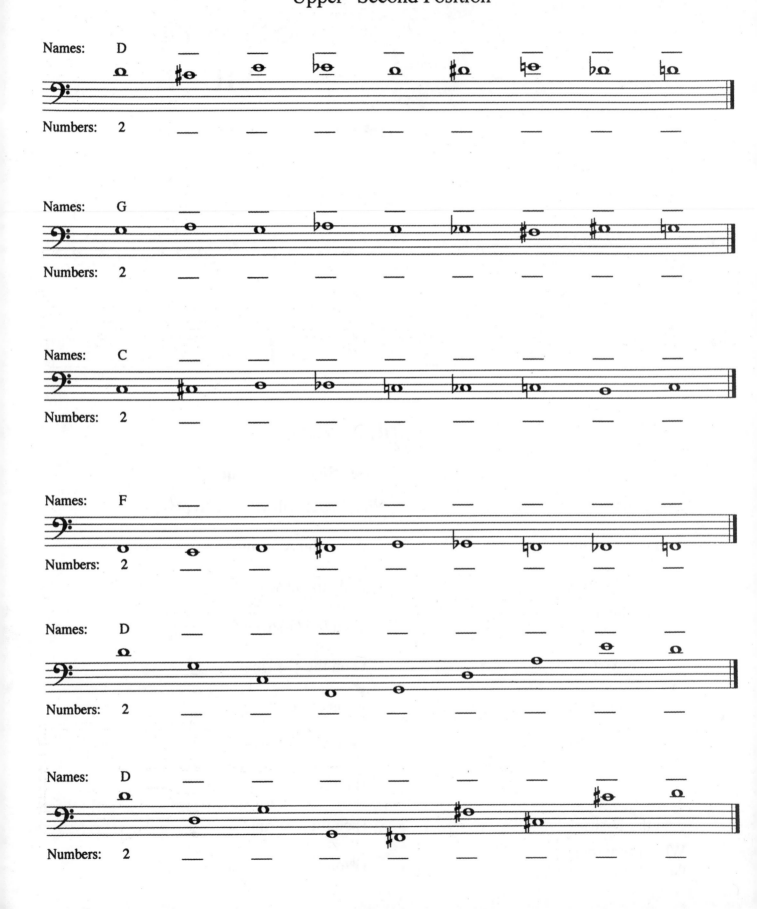

Fanfare

Skating

The Elephant's Waltz

The Tired Tortoise

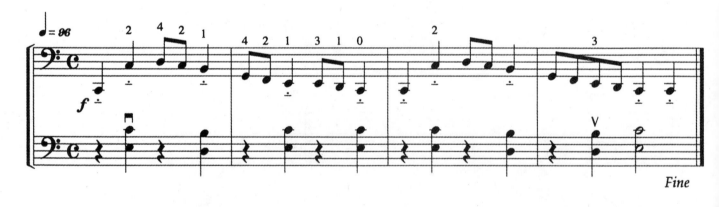

Fine

D. C. al Fine

The Whale's Song

March

Sitting in the Shade

Bugle Call

Toy Soldiers

Lament

12

The Invisible Target

* This harmonic can be played in three different places. See if you can find them all.

Pachyderm Parade

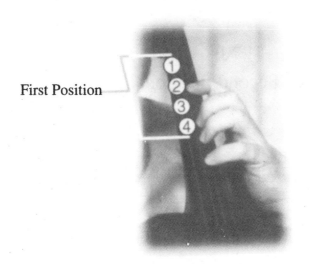

First Position

Extended Second Position

Target Practice

Geography Quiz

Your 2nd finger is on G on the D-string. Answer the following questions:

What note will be played by:

1 on the A-string? ____

x1 on the A-string? ____

3 on the G-string? ____

x1 on the D-string? ____

4 on the G-string? ____

x1 on the G-string? ____

What is another
name for that note? ____

What finger will you use to play:

G♯ on the D-string? ____

A♭ on the D-string? ____

E♭ on the C-string? ____

D on the G-string? ____

F on the C-string? ____

B on the G-string? ____

D on the A-string? ____

14

Names and Numbers
Extended Second Position

Names: D

Numbers: 2

Names: G

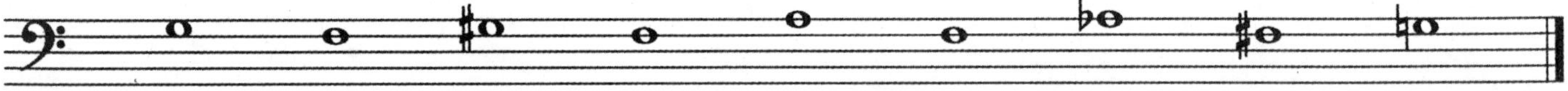

Numbers: 2

Names: C

Numbers: 2

Names: F

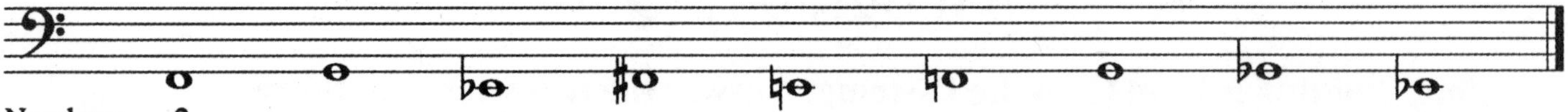

Numbers: 2

Names: G

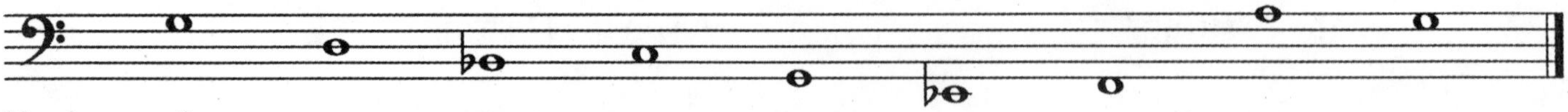

Numbers: 2

Names: C

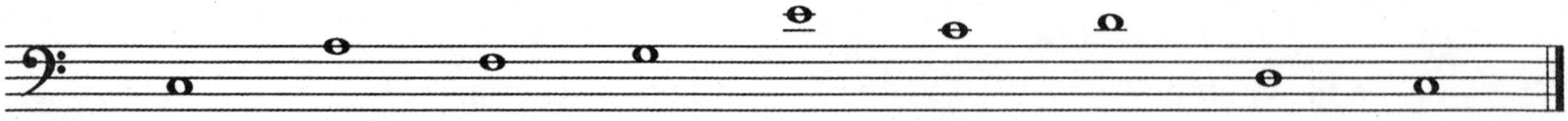

Numbers: 2

Ballad

C Song

Somersaults and Cartwheels

Tango

Erik's Minuet

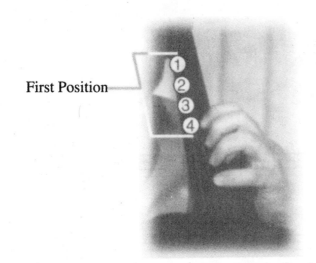

First Position

"Lower" Third Position

Target Practice

II   I   II   I   III   II   III   II   IV   III   IV   III

Geography Quiz

Your 1st finger is on D on the A-string. Answer the following questions:

What note will be played by:

1 on the C-string? ____

4 on the A-string? ____

3 on the G-string? ____

2 on the D-string? ____
What is another
name for that note? ____

1 on the G-string? ____

4 on the C-string? ____

3 on the A-string? ____

1 on the G-string? ____

What finger will you use to play:

E♭ on the A-string? ____

G on the C-string? ____

C♯ on the G-string? ____

F♯ on the C-string? ____

E♭ on the G-string? ____

B♭ on the D-string? ____

A♭ on the C-string? ____

G♯ on the C-string? ____

A on the D-string? ____

Names and Numbers
"Lower" Third Position

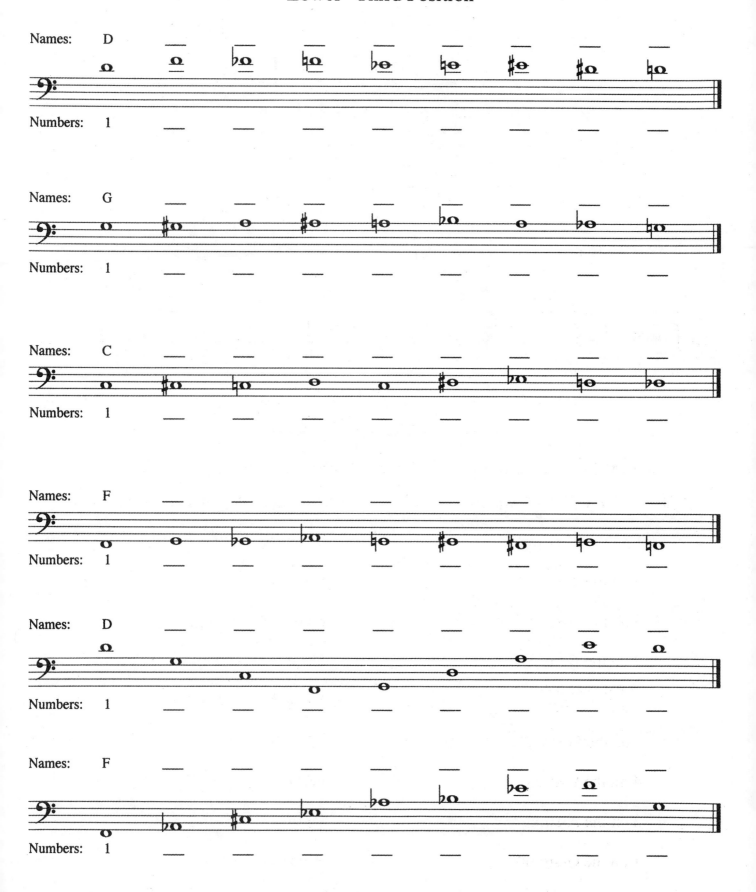

Japanese Garden

I'm So Sleepy

March of the Dinosaurs

The Haunted House

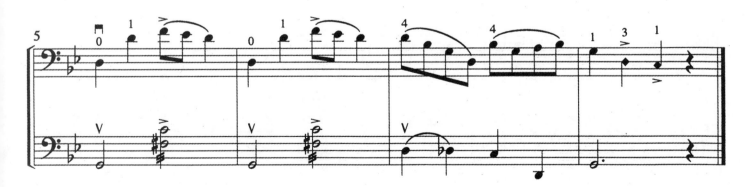

I Was a Teenage Monster

Fine

D. C. al Fine

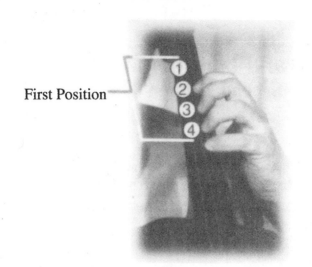

First Position

"Lower" Second Position

Target Practice

Geography Quiz

Your 3rd finger is on C on the G-string. Answer the following questions:

What note will be played by:

3 on the A-string? ____

4 on the A-string? ____

2 on the C-string? ____

1 on the D-string? ____

2 on the G-string? ____

3 on the C-string? ____

4 on the D-string? ____

What is another
name for that note? ____

1 on the A-string? ____

What finger will you use to play:

E♭ on the C-string? ____

C♯ on the G-string? ____

C♯ on the A-string? ____

B♭ on the G-string? ____

G on the D-string? ____

F♯ on the C-string? ____

F♯ on the D-string? ____

C on the G-string? ____

C on the A-string? ____

24

Names and Numbers
"Lower" Second Position

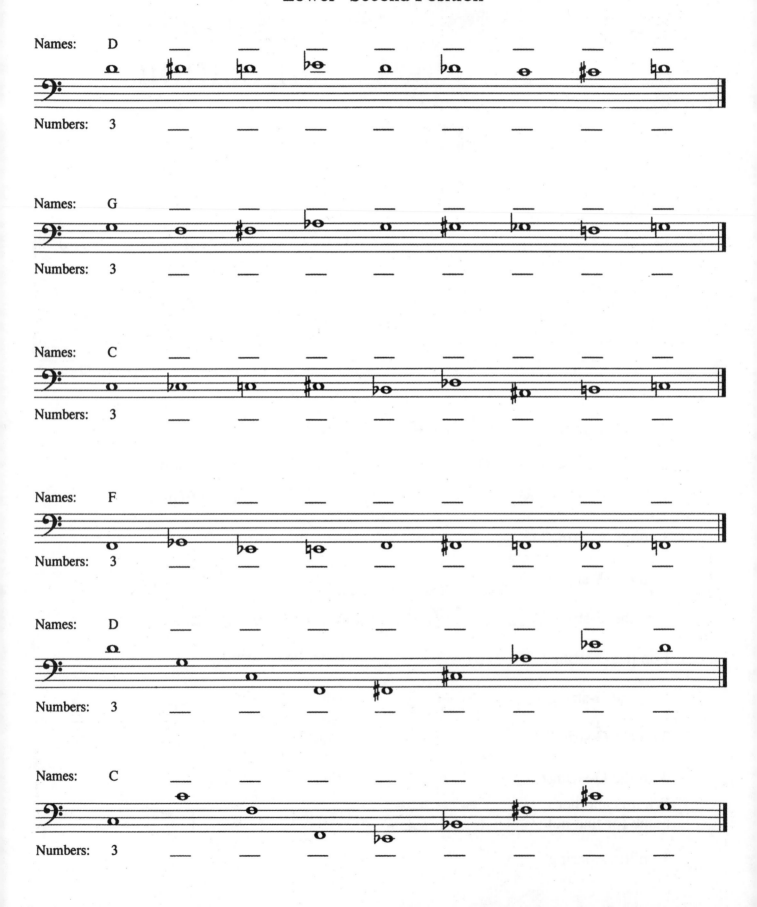

I've Got Homework

Valse Triste

Sicilienne

Etude

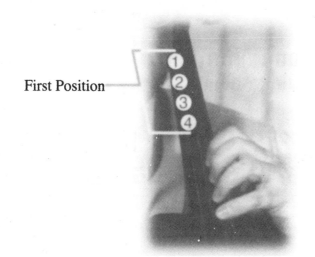

First Position

Fourth Position

Target Practice

Geography Quiz

Your 1st finger is on G on the C-string. Answer the following questions:

What note will be played by:

4 on the A-string? ____

2 on the D-string? ____

3 on the G-string? ____

1 on the A-string? ____

3 on the C-string? ____

1 on the D-string? ____

2 on the C-string? ____

What is another
name for that note? ____

4 on the D-string? ____

What finger will you use to play:

F♯ on the A-string? ____

D♯ on the G-string? ____

B♭ on the C-string? ____

F on the G-string? ____

B on the D-string? ____

E♭ on the G-string? ____

F on the A-string? ____

A♯ on the D-string? ____

G♭ on the A-string? ____

30

Names and Numbers
Fourth Position

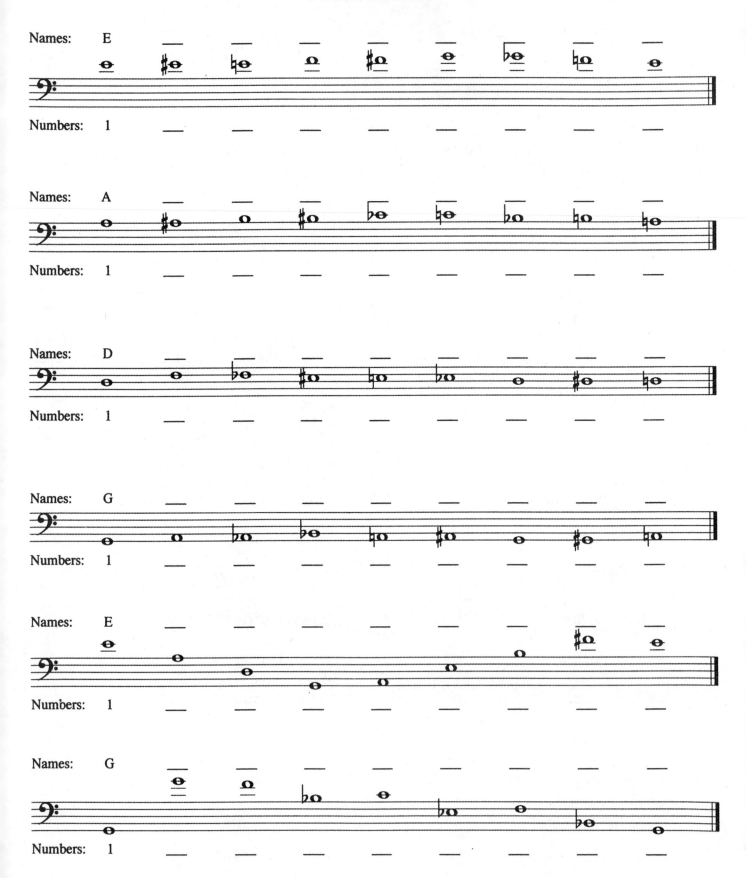

Church Bells

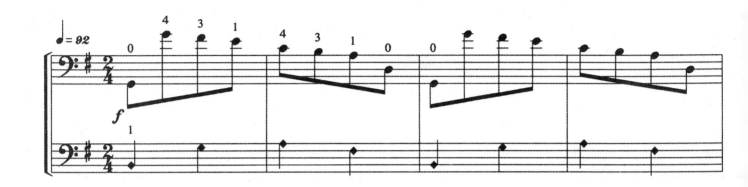

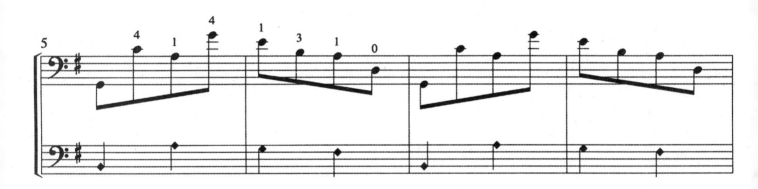

A Minor Melody

The Big Kangaroo

A Cloudy Day

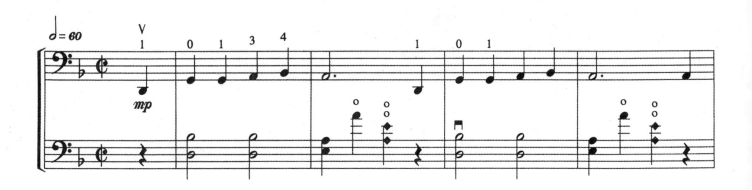

Busy Bees

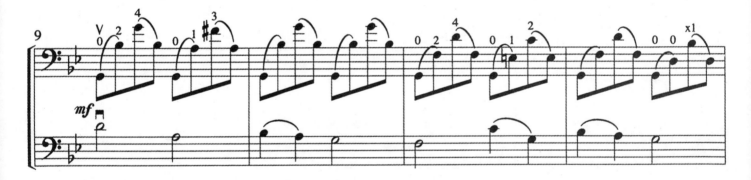

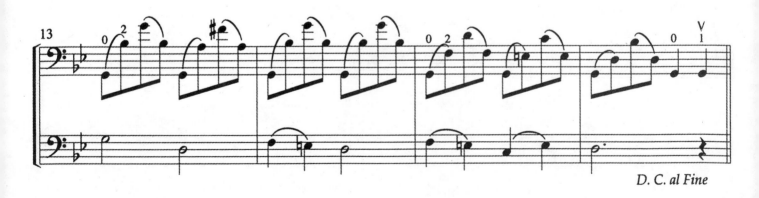

In A Hurry

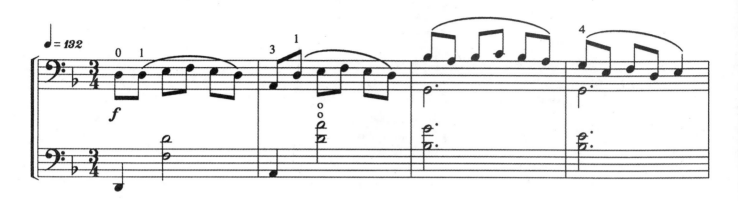

Fine

D. C. al Fine

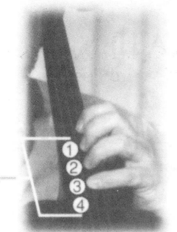

Fourth Position

"Upper" Third Position

Target Practice

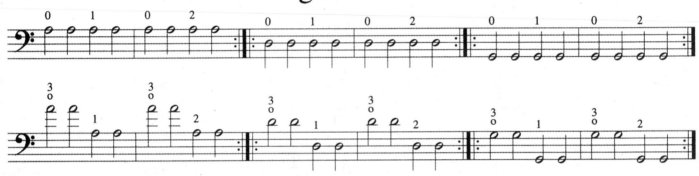

Geography Quiz

Your 2nd finger is on D on the G-string. Answer the following questions:

What note will be played by:

2 on the A-string? ____

1 on the C-string? ____

1 on the G-string? ____

1 on the D-string? ____

What is another
name for that note? ____

4 on the C-string? ____

4 on the G-string? ____

4 on the D-string? ____

4 on the A-string? ____

What finger will you use to play:

F on the A-string? ____

B♭ on the D-string? ____

E♭ on the G-string? ____

G# on the C-string? ____

A on the D-string? ____

G on the C-string? ____

E♭ on the A-string? ____

C# on the G-string? ____

F# on the C-string? ____

Names and Numbers
"Upper" Third Position

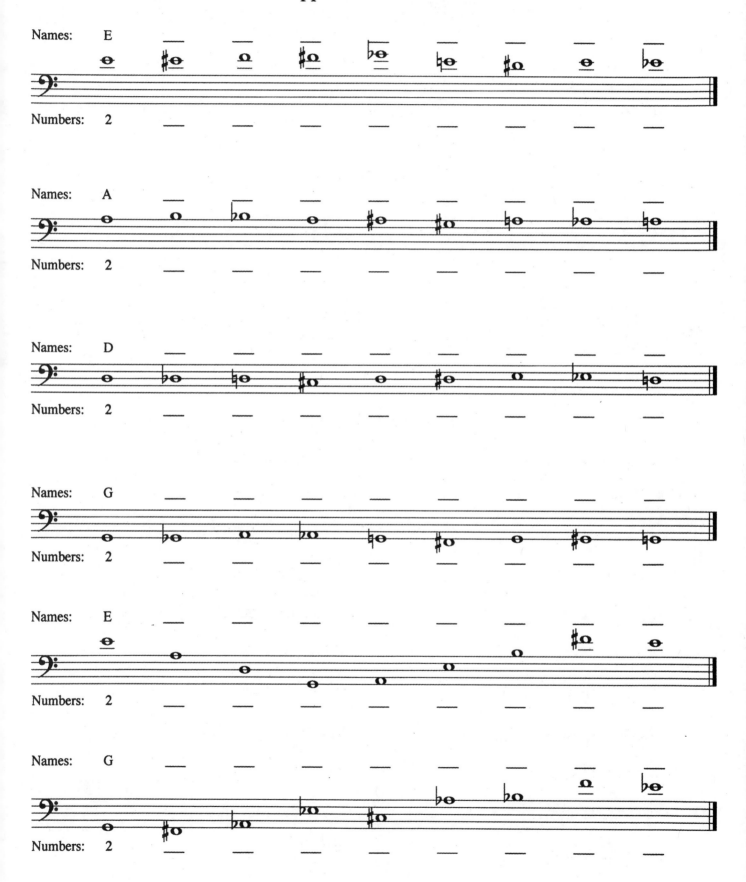

The Troubadour

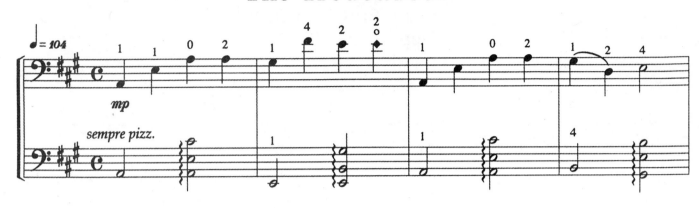

* see the note on "The Invisible Target"

Hoedown

A Waltz

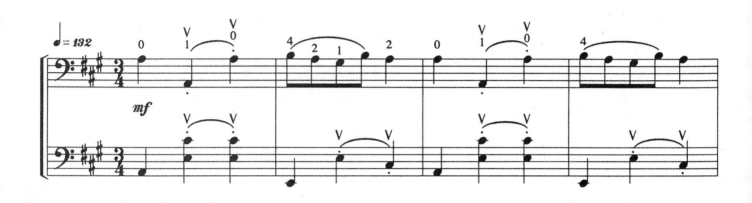

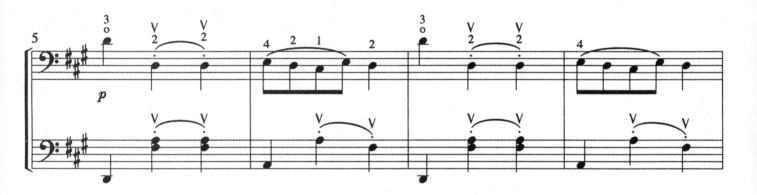

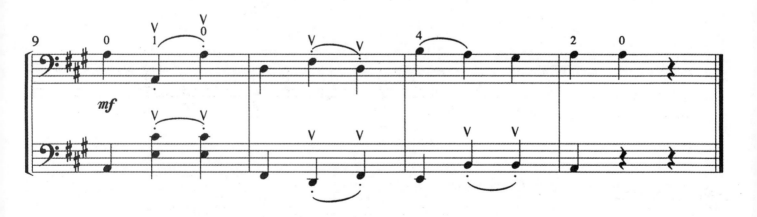

The Hippopotamus' Dance

The Heavy Highlander

Barcarole

42

Extended Third Position

Fourth Position

Target Practice

Geography Quiz

Your 2nd finger is on G on the C-string. Answer the following questions:

What note will be played by:

1 on the C-string? ____

x1 on the C-string? ____

2 on the G-string? ____

x1 on the D-string? ____

3 on the A-string? ____

1 on the D-string? ____

What is another
name for that note? ____

What finger will you use to play:

C on the G-string? ____

A♭ on the C-string? ____

E♭ on the A-string? ____

D on the A-string? ____

A on the D-string? ____

A on the C-string? ____

C♯ on the G-string? ____

Names and Numbers
Extended Third Position

Names: E

Numbers: 2

Names: A

Numbers: 2

Names: D

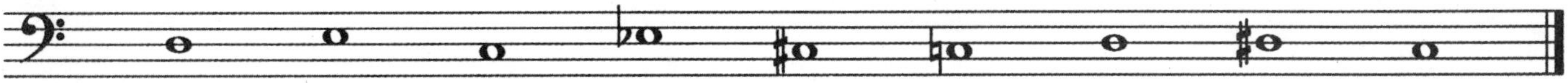

Numbers: 2

Names: G

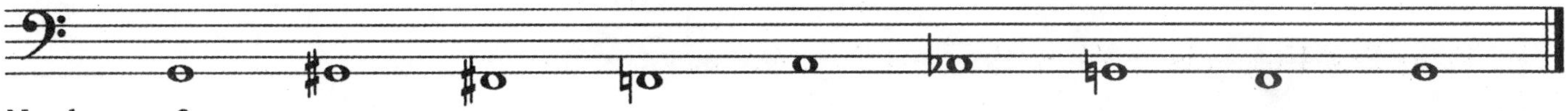

Numbers: 2

Names: E

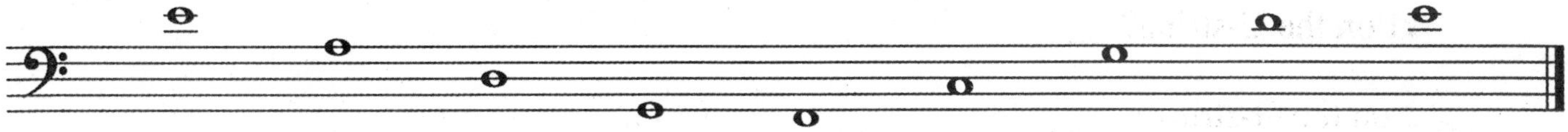

Numbers: 2

Names: A

Numbers: 2

44

Dreamland

Marching Martians

Bugle Call

Note: "Toy Soldiers" also can be fingered in third position.

The Tiny Ballerina

Jig

Fine

D. C. al Fine

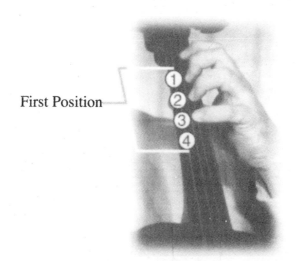

First Position

Half Position

Target Practice

Geography Quiz

Your 2nd finger is on B on the A-string. Answer the following questions:

What note will be played by:

    1 on the A-string? ____

    What is another
    name for that note? ____

    1 on the D-string? ____

    What is another
    name for that note? ____

    1 on the G-string? ____

    What is another
    name for that note? ____

    1 on the C-string? ____

    What is another
    name for that note? ____

    4 on the A-string? ____

What finger will you use to play:

    F♯ on the D-string? ____

    B on the G-string? ____

    E on the C-string? ____

    A on the G-string? ____

    B♭ on the G-string? ____

    E♭ on the C-string? ____

    D♯ on the C-string? ____

    C on the A-string? ____

    F on the D-string? ____

Names and Numbers
Half Position

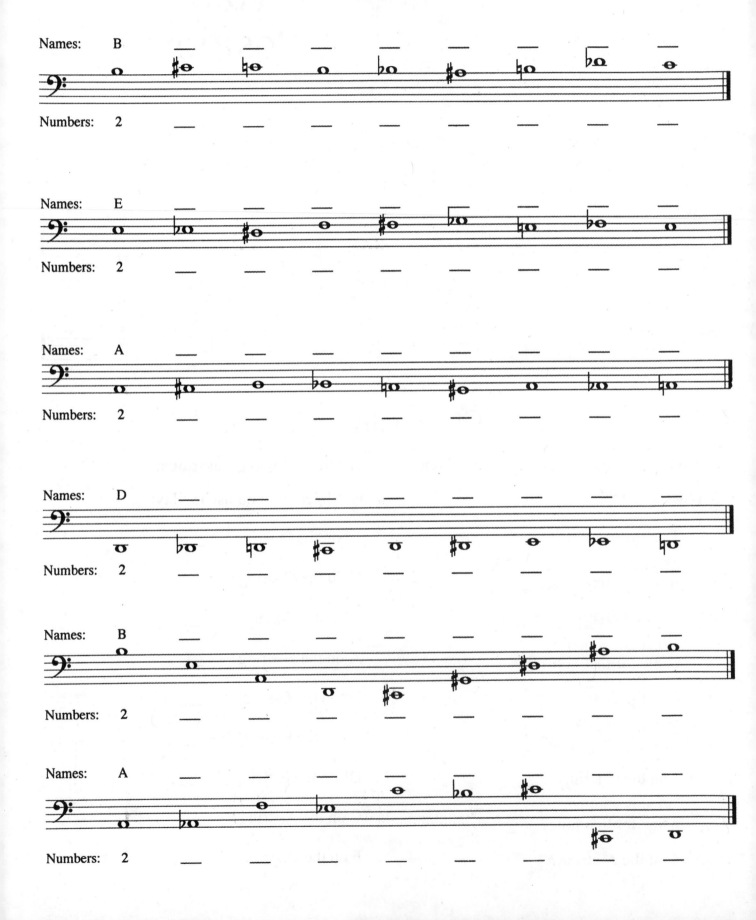

Half Position Serenade

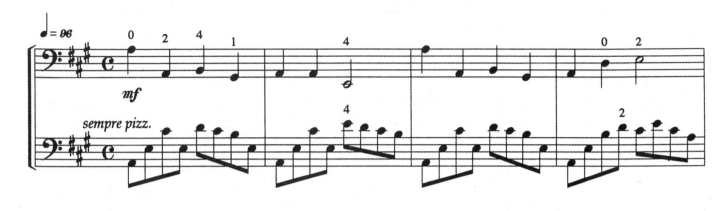

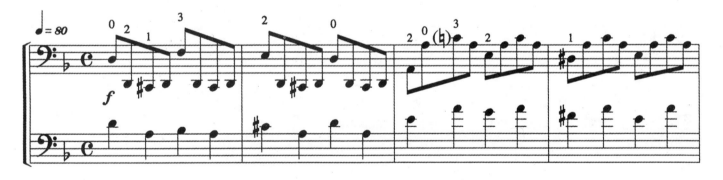

The Shark

Running

Fine

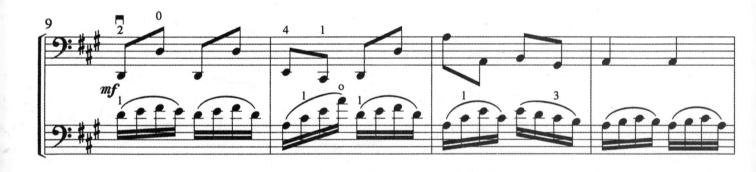

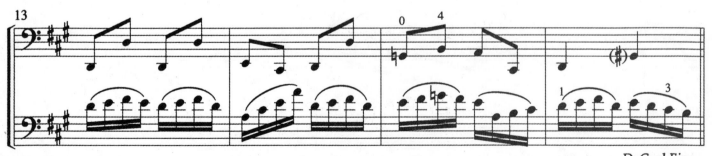

D. C. al Fine

Going Baroque

Spanish Dance

At The Ball

Sad Song

Walking Home

Ländler

Feeling Fine

D. C. al Fine

The Irish Tenor

Melancholy

Jack Spratt Dances with His Wife

Fine

Jack Spratt Dances with His Wife -- page 2

D. C. al Fine

Playing in the Park

Fine

D. C. al Fine

I Got the Blues, Baby